Underground to Canada
Lit Link

Grades 4-6

Written by Judith Wearing, Ph.D., B.Ed.
Illustrated by S&S Learning Materials

About the author: Judith Wearing is an award-winning educator, author, and multi-media designer who has taught on two continents. She has worked in the informal education system and as an education consultant, and is now entrenched in publishing.

ISBN 978-1-55035-898-8
Copyright 2007
All Rights Reserved * Printed in Canada

Published in the United States by:
On The Mark Press
3909 Witmer Road PMB 175
Niagara Falls, New York
14305
www.onthemarkpress.com

Published in Canada by:
S&S Learning Materials
15 Dairy Avenue
Napanee, Ontario
K7R 1M4
www.sslearning.com

At a Glance

Learning Expectations

Learning Expectations	Chapters 1-2	Chapters 3-4	Chapters 5-6	Chapters 7-8	Chapters 9-10	Chapters 11-12	Chapters 13-14	Chapters 15-16	Chapter 17	Chapter 18	Chapter 19
Reading Comprehension											
• Identify and describe story elements	•	•	•	•	•	•	•	•	•	•	•
• Summarize events and details	•	•	•	•	•	•	•	•	•	•	•
Reasoning & Critical Thinking Skills											
• Character traits, comparisons					•	•	•				•
• Use context clues		•	•	•	•				•	•	•
• Make inferences (e.g., why events occurred, characters' thoughts and feelings, etc.)	•	•	•	•	•	•	•	•	•	•	•
• Determine the meaning of colloquialisms and other phrases		•	•		•			•			
• Understand abstract concepts (e.g., grief, loss, friendship, family, loyalty, prejudice, etc.)	•	•	•	•	•		•	•	•	•	•
• Develop opinions and personal interpretations	•	•	•	•	•	•	•	•	•	•	•
• Write a biography							•				
• Write a letter/editorial for a newspaper										•	
• Develop research skills	•	•	•		•	•	•	•			
• Create a book cover or drawing						•		•			
• Create a map										•	
• Create a song/secret signal		•			•		•				
Vocabulary Development, Grammar & Word Use											
• Identify setting	•				•						
• Identify synonyms and antonyms		•	•		•		•				
• Identify similes and metaphors	•	•					•				•
• Identify suffixes and prefixes						•					
• Identify syllables	•										
• Identify descriptive words and phrases		•		•			•	•	•		•
• Identify parts of speech		•		•							
• Develop dictionary skills	•	•			•	•					
• Use words correctly in sentences		•	•							•	
• Place words in alphabetical order							•				
• Identify singular/plural									•		
• Identify root words						•					
• Use capitals and punctuation correctly					•						
• Visualize vocabulary		•	•					•			

Underground to Canada
By Barbara Smucker

Table of Contents

Underground to Canada

By Barbara Smucker

Overall Expectations

The students will:

- develop their skills in reading, writing, listening, and oral communication

- use good literature as a vehicle for developing skills required by curriculum expectations: reasoning and critical thinking, knowledge of language structure, vocabulary building, and use of conventions

- become meaningfully engaged in the drama of literature through a variety of types of questions and activities

- identify and describe elements of stories (e.g., plot, main idea, characters, setting)

- learn and review many skills in order to develop good reading habits

- provide clear answers to questions and well-constructed explanations

- organize and classify information to clarify thinking

- learn about the history of slavery in the United States

- learn about the abstract concepts of prejudice, terror, injustice, kindness, pride, and courage

- relate events and feelings found in novels to their own lives and experiences

- appreciate the importance of friendship and loyalty in personal relationships

- learn the importance of dealing with adversity and developing perseverance in the face of adversity

- state their own interpretation of a written work, using evidence from the work and from their own knowledge and experience

- learn to accept and understand the horrors of slavery, the range of human behaviors from good to evil, and the importance of self-esteem

Teacher Suggestions

This unit can be used in a variety of ways:

1. The student booklet focuses for the most part on one chapter of the novel at a time. Each of the sections contains the following activities:
   a) Before you read the chapter (reasoning and critical thinking skills)
   b) Vocabulary (dictionary and thesaurus skills)
   c) Questions (reading comprehension skills)
   d) Language Activities (grammar, punctuation, and word structure)

2. Students may read the novel at their own speed and then select, or be assigned, a variety of questions and activities.

3. Bulletin Board and Interest Center Ideas: Themes might include Mississippi, Canada, railroads, slavery, friendship, bravery.

4. Pre-Reading Activities. *Underground to Canada* can also be used in conjunction with social studies themes involving the history of slavery in the United States, and emotional development themes of prejudice, friendship, pride, and bravery.

Underground to Canada
By Barbara Smucker

5. Independent Reading Approach: Students who are able to work independently may attempt to complete the assignments in a self-directed manner. Initially, these students should participate in the pre-reading activities with the rest of the class. Students should familiarize themselves with the reproducible student booklet. Completed worksheets should be submitted so that the teacher can note how quickly and accurately the students are working. Students may be brought together periodically to discuss issues in specific sections of the novel.

6. Fine Art Activities: Students may investigate traditional slavery songs, and birds and flowers of the deep South, Canadian and deep South climates.

7. Encourage the students to keep a reading log in which they record their reading each day and their thoughts about the passage.

8. Students should keep all their work together in one place. A portfolio cover is provided for this purpose.

9. Students should not be expected to complete all activities. Teachers should allow choice and in some cases match the activity to the student's ability.

10. Students should keep track (in their portfolio) of the activities they complete.

List of Activities

Vocabulary Development

1. Identify similes and metaphors
2. Locate descriptive words/phrases
3. Use plurals correctly
4. Use capitals and punctuation correctly
5. Identify syllables
6. Use a dictionary
7. Visualize vocabulary words
8. Use content clues
9. Identify parts of speech
10. Determine alphabetical order
11. Identify prefixes and suffixes

Setting Activities

1. Summarize the details of a setting
2. Draw a setting
3. Compare and contrast settings

Plot Activities

1. Chart a map of movements
2. Sequence events

Character Activities

1. Determine character traits
2. Compare characters
3. Understand concepts such as bravery and self-respect
4. Make inferences about characters' emotions and reactions

Creative and Critical Thinking

1. Reflect on personal opinions
2. Write descriptions of personal feelings
3. Write an editorial
4. Develop research skills
5. Discuss issues with classmates

Art Activities

1. Design a cover for the novel
2. Draw vocabulary and setting
3. Create a song

Underground to Canada
By Barbara Smucker

Synopsis

Julilly is a young girl, and a slave. She lives on a cotton plantation in Virginia – until she's sold and taken to Mississippi, where the food is scarce and the slave boss is very mean. She befriends Liza, a girl who is badly crippled from her beatings, and the two decide to escape to a country they've heard about where slaves are free: Canada. When a white man from Canada arrives and secretly gives them information about how to make the trip, the plan is sealed. Four slaves run away, two are caught. Liza and Julilly are helped many times by a group of people that are known as the Underground Railroad, transporting "packages" safely across the border. Will Liza and Julilly escape the slave hunters and bloodhounds that are tracking them down to reach a place where they can hold their heads up high?

Author Biography
Barbara Smucker

It was at age 11 that Barbara Smucker decided to be an author. She was living in a small town in Kansas at the time, where she was born in 1915. She stayed in Kansas and went to university there, and then moved to Canada with her husband who got a job working at a Mennonite college in Ontario. Barbara had many careers: she was a newspaper reporter, a teacher, and a librarian, as well as an author. She has written many books, often telling the stories of children who have been overlooked by other authors. Her best known books include *Henry's Red Sea* (1955), *Cherokee Run* (1957), *Wigwam in the City* (1966), *Days of Terror* (1979), *Amish Adventure* (1983), *Jacob's little Giant* (1987), *Selina and the Bearpaw Quit* (1995), and *Selina and the Shoe-Fly Pie* (1998).

Underground to Canada
By Barbara Smucker

Student Checklist

Student Name: _____

Assignment	Grade/Level	Comments

Underground to Canada

By Barbara Smucker

Name:_____

Underground to Canada
By Barbara Smucker

Chapter 1

Before you read:

In the forward to this book, there is a passage from a speech by Martin Luther King Jr. Martin Luther King Jr. is an important figure in the history of black people in America. Do some research to find out why.

_____

_____

_____

_____

Vocabulary:

Divide the following words into syllables. For example: **Ju/lil/ly**

plantation _____

overseer _____

Virginia _____

melody _____

quarters _____

trader _____

Massa _____

chirping _____

Questions:

1. What does Massa mean?_____

2. Why didn't Massa Hensen like Mammy Sally's song?

_____

_____

Underground to Canada

By Barbara Smucker

3. What is happening to the Hensens and their plantation?

_____

_____

4. What are the slaves on the Hensen plantation nervous about?

_____

_____

5. What is 'Julilly' short form for?

_____

Language Activities:

1. The setting of a novel describes the place and the time. What is the setting of *Underground to Canada*?

_____

_____

2. Research the plantations of the southern United States in the last century. How big were they? What did they grow? Who owned them? Who worked on them?

_____

_____

_____

_____

_____

Underground to Canada
By Barbara Smucker

Chapter 2

Before you read:

In the plantations of the deep South, black people were kept as slaves. In your own words, describe what slave means (use a dictionary if you need help).

_____

_____

Imagine how you would feel to be a slave.

_____

_____

_____

Vocabulary:

Using a dictionary, write a definition for each of the following.

calloused: _____

hobble:_____

mulatto: _____

buttermilk: _____

hoecake:_____

Questions:

1. What does the old ram horn do?_____

2. What did the slaves on the Hensen plantation eat for breakfast?

Underground to Canada
By Barbara Smucker

3. What is the fat man doing at the Hensen plantation?

_____

4. **a)** What did the fat man do to Julilly? _____

   b) How did this make her feel?

   _____

5. List the slaves that were taken away from the Hensen plantation.

   _____

   _____

6. Why are the men bound in chains?

   _____

Language Activities:

1. **a)** In Chapter Two, the slaves are bought and sold like animals. Tell what you think of this.

   _____

   _____

   b) Is it wrong to treat people this way? Explain.

   _____

   _____

   _____

Underground to Canada

By Barbara Smucker

2. The word 'nigger' is not a nice word. Describe the situation in which the word is used by the fat man in this chapter.

   _____

   _____

   _____

3. The author says, "the chain became a silver snake". This is an example of a metaphor. A **metaphor** is a comparison between two objects to help describe something. In this example, the chain is compared to a silver snake. Think of a metaphor to describe the following.

   the fat man's whip: _____

   _____

   the wagon: _____

   _____

   mud: _____

   _____

Underground to Canada
By Barbara Smucker

Chapter 3

Before you read:

In this chapter, Julilly is taken away on a wagon, her future unknown. Describe a time when there was a change in your life and your future was unknown.

_____

_____

How did you feel at this time of uncertainty?

_____

_____

Vocabulary:

Write sentences using each of these words or phrases to show their meaning. Use a dictionary to help you.

clang: _____

_____

mirage: _____

_____

skimpy: _____

_____

gourd: _____

_____

Quaker: _____

_____

Underground to Canada
By Barbara Smucker

Abolitionist: _____

_____

Questions:

1. What was the "sheets of falling water" the children saw? _____

2. What caused the blood on Lester's legs?

   _____

3. How was the young black boy at the water different than Julilly?

   _____

4. What did the black boy give Julilly? _____

5. Why did the fat man not like the slaves talking to the young black boy and the white man at the stream?

   _____

   _____

Language Activities:

1. The author says, "the clang of the chained men behind it took up a rhythm... it was a slow, sad rhythm – sad as the bells tolling a death from the village church." This is an example of a **simile**, which is a comparison using **like** or **as**. In this example, the sound of the chain gang is compared to the sound of a bell announcing death. Think of similes to describe the following.

   the fat man's whip: _____

   _____

Underground to Canada

By Barbara Smucker

the wagon: _____

_____

mud: _____

_____

2. Do some research about Quakers.

   a) How did they dress in the 19th century?

   _____

   _____

   b) What are some main ideas Quakers believe in?

   _____

   _____

   _____

Underground to Canada
By Barbara Smucker

Chapter 4

Before you read:

If someone hits you on purpose, your feelings can be hurt as well as your body. How would you feel if somebody hit you on purpose?

_____

_____

_____

Vocabulary:

Circle the **synonym** (the word with the same meaning) for each underlined word in the sentence.

1. The **clattering** of the wagon boards let them know they were traveling again.

    nails   racket   wheels   paint   music

2. I **yearned** for happier days.

    asked   loved   wanted   tried   wrote

3. The **stifling** heat made it difficult to work.

    lovely   gentle   nasty   extra   unbearable

4. The **clanging** of the bell called us to dinner.

    moving   swaying   ringing   singing   louchess

5. After being stung by a bee, his finger was **swollen**.

    hurting   broken   puffy   red   uncomfortable

Underground to Canada
By Barbara Smucker

Questions:

1. How did Julilly comfort the children in the wagon?

2. Did the rain make it harder or easier for the slaves? Explain your answer.

3. What did Julilly do that was brave?

4. **a)** How did Lester respond to Julilly's bravery?

   b) How did this make Julilly feel?

Language Activities:

1. This chapter has lots of **adjectives**: words that describe objects. How many can you find? Try to find at least 10.

2. Many emotions are felt by the slaves in this chapter. Describe a situation in which you might feel each of these emotions.

hatred:_____

_____

pride:_____

_____

fear: _____

_____

anger: _____

_____

approval: _____

_____

Extension:

Sing the song at the end of this chapter. Do some research to see if you can find out where this song originated.

_____

_____

_____

_____

_____

Underground to Canada
By Barbara Smucker

Chapter 5

Before you read:

In this chapter, the wagon arrives at its destination. Describe a time when you went on a trip, and arrived at your destination. What were your first thoughts?

_____

_____

_____

Vocabulary:

Choose a word from the list to compete each sentence.

fragrance	pillars	plume	sagged	sullen
appraised	parading	sprouted	drawled	billows

1. The woman's voice _____ with an accent that identified her as southern.

2. _____ of cloud filled the sky, like fluffy cotton wool.

3. The _____ of the flowers filled the dining room.

4. We watched as a _____ of smoke rose from the fire.

5. After several days, the seeds we had planted _____ from the earth.

6. Grandmother looked _____ as she watched the soldiers on the television news.

7. My sister and I were _____ about in our best clothes when our guests arrived.

8. The old roof _____ in the middle, and gave the house an unstable appearance.

9. I _____ the job I'd done cleaning my room, and was satisfied.

10. The entire building was surrounded by a huge porch that was held up with round, white _____.

Questions:

1. What state is the destination of the wagon?_____

2. What was the name of the fat man, and what was his job on the plantation?

   _____

3. The other slaves on the Riley plantation are not kind to the newcomers. Why do you think this is?

   _____

   _____

   _____

Language Activies:

1. The lawn of the Riley plantation is covered in magnolia trees. Do some research about the magnolia tree, and draw and color a picture of a magnolia flower.

Underground to Canada
By Barbara Smucker

Chapter 6

Before you read:

In this chapter, Julilly hears about things that have happened to Liza that are very upsetting. "It squeezed her throat and made her breathing come in jumps." Think of something terrible you have heard about. How did it make you feel?

_____

_____

_____

Vocabulary:

Circle the word in each line that does not belong and write a sentence to explain why it does not fit.

1.	strong	healthy	robust	frail	resilient
2.	misery	gaiety	unhappiness	sadness	hopelessness
3.	tense	anxious	relaxed	busy	agitated
4.	sharp	piercing	stabbing	blunt	acute
5.	glistening	dull	drab	flat	shadowed

Underground to Canada
By Barbara Smucker

Questions:

1. What is Julilly's first impression of Liza?

2. Why does Liza have beat up legs and a bent up back?

3. What did Julilly see in the morning that shocked her?

4. Describe what the slaves ate for breakfast and lunch?

Language Activities:

1. What did Liza's dad mean when he said, "Liza, the soul is all black or white 'pending on the man's life and not on his skin."

2. Research cotton.

   a) What is cotton used for? Where does it grow?

   b) What is a cotton boll?

Underground to Canada
By Barbara Smucker

c) Describe how it was gathered during the times of the slave plantations, and compare this to how it is gathered today. Draw a picture to accompany your comparisons.

How Cotton Was Gathered on Slave Plantations

How Cotton Is Gathered Today

Underground to Canada

By Barbara Smucker

Chapter 7

Before you read:

In this chapter, Julilly and Liza meet a stranger who they find very interesting. Describe a time that you met a stranger you found interesting. What do you remember about the way they looked and talked?

_____

_____

_____

Vocabulary:

Find the words below in this word search puzzle.

cotton	
Riley	
cat-o-nine-tails	
lashes	
Tennessee	
plantation	
Sims	
mosquitoes	
ornithologist	
shotgun	
scientific	
Julilly	
noonday	
magnolia	
Canada	
furrows	

```
l l n h b c a g m m n n z q r
j i a i l o n g a m t o r m n
s i m s l m o s q u i t o e s
u j s m e o r a p p l l b v f
l y c a t o n i n e t a i l s
l p i t s s i o u v r r w w o
y o e n t o t b r c c s o w c
a t n n w t h k u g s r r n a
d e t t o q o r j h r i g b n
n o i c r u l o o u s l l i a
o j f t f i o t f q h e a g l
o u i s s t g n u n l y n n a
n l c m a u i r o k l a t s s
r i l i n l s t t o p l n n h
r l e s g t t e n n e s s e e
o l y m n o i t a t n a l p s
c y h s c a n a d a d y a m s
```

Underground to Canada
By Barbara Smucker

Questions:

1. How much cotton did each slave pick every day?

    _____

2. What happened if a slave did not pick enough cotton?

    _____

3. Describe the stories the slaves had heard about Canada.

    _____

    _____

    _____

    _____

4. What was Mr. Alexander Ross doing at the Riley plantation?

    _____

5. Why do you think Julilly stared at Mr. Ross like she did?

    _____

    _____

Language Activities:

1. Brainstorm as many words as you can that end in "ogist" – like "ornithologist". Try to find at least six.

    _____   _____   _____

    _____   _____   _____

    _____   _____   _____

Underground to Canada

By Barbara Smucker

2. Prejudice happens when someone is treated in a negative way because of what they look like, the clothes they wear, their customs and traditions, or their families. With a partner, discuss examples of prejudice that have happened to you or people you know.

_____

_____

_____

_____

_____

_____

_____

_____

_____

_____

3. a) Have you ever shown prejudice towards other people?

_____

_____

_____

b) Why does prejudice happen?

_____

_____

_____

Underground to Canada
By Barbara Smucker

Chapter 8

Before you read:

To Julilly and Liza, Canada means freedom. What does Canada mean to you?

_____

_____

Vocabulary:

Draw a straight line from the vocabulary word to its definition. Use a straight edge, such as a ruler.

a)	roused	moving swiftly and lightly
b)	spark	skinny
c)	flitting	particular way of speaking
d)	flicker	awakened
e)	scant	neat and tidy
f)	orderly	rough sounding
g)	accent	jerk
h)	scrawny	a small, sudden flash of light
i)	twitch	shine irregularly
j)	hoarsely	not enough

Questions:

1. What doesn't grow in Canada? _____

2. Why did the arrival of Mr. Ross "unsettle" the slaves?

_____

_____

3. What is the significance of the North Star to the slaves?

_____

_____

4. What does freedom mean to Julilly?

_____

_____

5. What did the girls pledge to do at the end of this chapter?

_____

Language Activities:

1. Find five adjectives, five verbs, five nouns, and five adverbs from this chapter.

Verbs	Adverbs	Adjectives	Nouns
e.g., coming	too	amazing	crop
_____	_____	_____	_____
_____	_____	_____	_____
_____	_____	_____	_____
_____	_____	_____	_____
_____	_____	_____	_____

2. Draw a picture of the "drinking gourd" stars also known as "the big dipper". Label the North Star.

Underground to Canada
By Barbara Smucker

Chapter 9

Before you read:

A whippoorwill is a bird that plays an important role in this book. Do some research to find out about the whippoorwill. Where does it live? When does it sing? And what does its song sound like?

_____

_____

_____

_____

_____

Vocabulary:

For each of the words in the table, guess at the definition. Then look each one up in the dictionary. Put a check mark beside those words you guessed correctly.

Word	Your Guess	Dictionary Definition
a) ruckus		
b) scrounged		
c) pledge		
d) solemn		
e) taut		
f) liberate		
g) wit		

Underground to Canada

By Barbara Smucker

Questions:

1. Use this Venn diagram to compare and contrast a Sunday at the Riley plantation and the Hensen plantation.

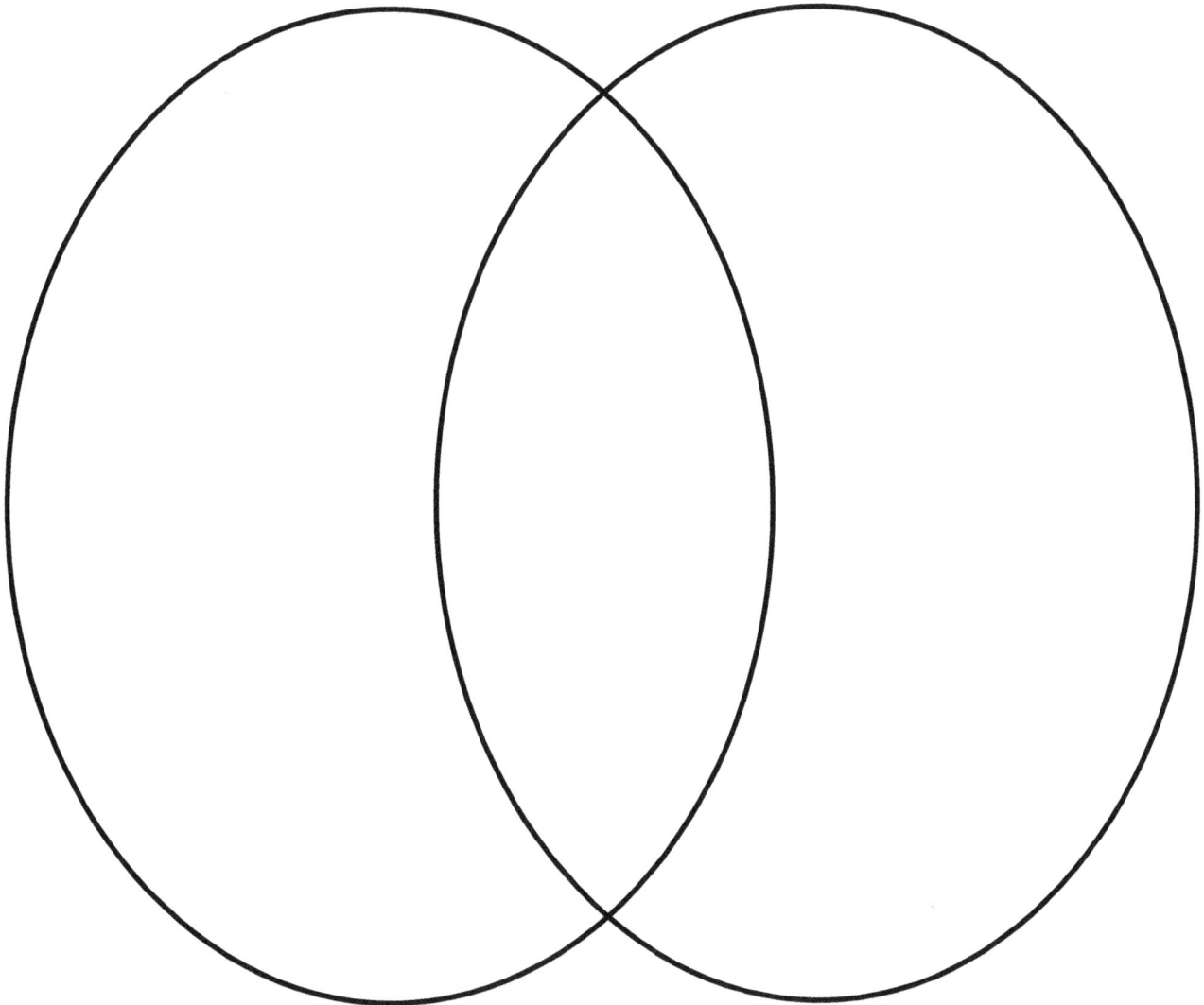

2. Why did Liza drop her stick?

_____

Underground to Canada
By Barbara Smucker

3. **a)** What did Julilly do when Liza dropped her stick?

_____

   b) What reason did Julilly have for doing this?

_____

_____

4. What did three calls of the whippoorwill signal?

_____

5. How did Mr. Ross greet Julilly and Liza in the woods?

_____

Language Activities:

1. Write the following sentences using correct punctuation and capitals.

   a) on sundays julilly and liza washed their clothes at the riley plantation

_____

   b) when bessie fell asleep the girls met lester in the woods

_____

   c) will the girls meet mr ross to talk about going to canada

_____

2. Mr. Ross is known as a "Negro Thief". What is your opinion about this?

_____

_____

_____

Underground to Canada
By Barbara Smucker

Chapter 10

Before you read:

Running away and being chased by bloodhounds is a frightening experience that the characters have to endure. Tell of an experience that would be frightening for you to endure.

_____

_____

Vocabulary:

Choose a vocabulary word that means the same or almost the same as the underlined words in the sentences below.

knapsack	sun high	grumble	lank
jovial	meagre	astonished	serene

1. I put my school supplies in my **backpack**.   _____

2. The slave did not **complain** about the heavy load
   on his back.   _____

3. Back stage, the actor was **surprised** to hear how loud
   the audience applauded.   _____

4. The slaves' **scant** supplies were barely enough to keep
   them alive.   _____

5. We will stop to rest at **noon**.   _____

6. His **happy** grin made us all feel relaxed.   _____

7. The celery was **limp** and soft.   _____

8. The water was calm and **peaceful**.   _____

Underground to Canada
By Barbara Smucker

Questions:

1. Julilly is nervous in this chapter, and the author gives the creatures around her the same nervous quality. Find two examples of creatures at the beginning of this chapter and write the words that the author uses to make them share in Julilly's nervousness.

   _____

   _____

2. Why was Julilly concerned about the approaching storm?

   _____

   _____

3. Why did Lester take a roundabout path through the woods?

   _____

4. What did Mr. Ross give the slaves?

   _____

5. Did the slaves sleep well the first night of their journey? Explain your answer.

   _____

   _____

Language Activities:

1. Julilly shows courage in this chapter. Find two passages in the novel to show this, and describe them here.

   _____

   _____

   _____

   _____

Underground to Canada

By Barbara Smucker

2. **a)** What items do Liza and Julilly store away for their journey?

    _____

    _____

    b) Write a list of items that you would bring with you if you had to survive in the wilderness.

    _____

    _____

    _____

3. The secret signal for Julilly and Liza to leave and meet Lester was the song of the whippoorwill, three times. Suppose you had to invent a secret signal for your friends to know it was time to leave. It should be a sound that is normally heard in your surroundings. Describe it here.

    _____

    _____

    _____

Underground to Canada
By Barbara Smucker

Chapter 11

Before you read:

1. The Fugitive Slave Act was a law that existed in the United States in the 1800s. Do some research on this law:

a) When did this law come into being? _____

b) What did the law say?

_____

_____

_____

_____

Vocabulary:

1. Write the root word beside each of these verbs from Chapter 11.

    a) quivered _____   **b)** jogged   _____

    c) plodding _____   **d)** clopping _____

    e) croaking _____   **f)** lapping   _____

    g) lapsed   _____   **h)** scuffling _____

Questions:

1. How will the slaves know when they reach Tennessee?

_____

Underground to Canada
By Barbara Smucker

2. What does Lester's ability to read tell you about Massa Hensen?

_____

_____

3. What is the password that Mr. Ross told the slaves to remember?

_____

4. What could happen to anyone that helps a slave?

_____

_____

5. Why didn't Mr. Ross meet them?

_____

_____

6. Describe what the Quaker Abolitionist does to help the slaves.

_____

_____

_____

Language Activities:

1. Desert is a word that has two meanings: **1)** a hot, sandy region, and **2)** to leave alone. Try to think of two other examples of words that have two different meanings and write brief definitions for each.

Word: _____

Definitions:

  1. _____

  2. _____

Underground to Canada
By Barbara Smucker

Word: _____

Definitions:

1. _____

2. _____

2. Julilly, Liza, Lester, and Adam have very different personalities, but all are admirable people. List three things you admire about each one of these characters.

Liza:_____

_____

_____

Lester: _____

_____

_____

Adam: _____

_____

_____

Underground to Canada

By Barbara Smucker

Chapter 12

Before you read:

Bloodhounds were used to track down escaped slaves and criminals throughout history. Do some research to find out about this breed of dog. What does it look like? Why was it used to track slaves? What are bloodhounds used for today?

_____

_____

_____

_____

_____

Vocabulary:

Write the root words of the following, and put the suffixes and prefixes in the appropriate column.

	Root Word	Suffix	Prefix
a) darkness	_____	_____	_____
b) crossly	_____	_____	_____
c) untangle	_____	_____	_____
d) thoughtful	_____	_____	_____
e) nervous	_____	_____	_____
f) Abolitionists	_____	_____	_____
g) freedom	_____	_____	_____
h) lapping	_____	_____	_____

Underground to Canada
By Barbara Smucker

Questions:

1. What did the driver of the wagon give the slaves to help them on their journey?

   _____

2. What direction did the driver tell them to go?

   _____

3. What did the group eat for lunch?

   _____

4. Describe what happened to Lester and Adam at the end of the chapter.

   _____

   _____

   _____

Language Activities:

1. Predict what will happen to the girls.

   _____

   _____

   _____

2. On a separate sheet of paper, draw a picture of the inside of the barn. Beside your picture, write three words to describe it.

Underground to Canada
By Barbara Smucker

Chapter 13

Before you read:

Locate the Appalachians on a map of the United States.

What direction do you go to get from the Mississippi River to the Appalachian Mountains?

_____

Vocabulary:

Put the following words in alphabetical order.

stern   _____

sweet   _____

shallow   _____

scant   _____

fragrance   _____

crippled   _____

ragged   _____

despair   _____

craggy   _____

Questions:

1. Put the following statements in the order in which they happened in this chapter.

    _____ Julilly knocked on a farmhouse door and asked for food.

    _____ The Mennonites gave the girls food and sent them on their way.

Underground to Canada
By Barbara Smucker

_____ A farmer found the girls in the field with the cows.

_____ The girls walked east to the mountains.

_____ A woman held a gun at Julilly and told her to leave.

_____ Julilly and Liza rested in a cave.

_____ Mennonite women helped Julilly and Liza wash.

_____ Julilly sang.

2. Describe the Mennonite village.

_____

_____

_____

_____

Language Activities:

1. **a)** Research Mennonites to find out five facts about the way they live.

_____

_____

_____

_____

_____

b) Why did the Mennonites leave Germany to come to North America?

_____

_____

Underground to Canada

By Barbara Smucker

5. I was amazed at the sight of the **ancient** ruins in the field.

   historical   old   modern   past   creative

6. Her **wise** old eyes told me to stay still.

   smart   intelligent   clever   silly   experienced

Questions:

1. How did the girls protect themselves from the storm?

   _____

   _____

   _____

2. Why was the gift of bread from the old man so valuable?

   _____

   _____

3. What did the man with the dog tell Liza and Julilly to do?

   _____

   _____

4. Julilly and Liza were afraid to trust the man, but they did what he said anyway. Why?

   _____

5. a) What is the Underground Railway?

   _____

   _____

Underground to Canada

By Barbara Smucker

b) What are each of these things in the Underground Railway:

railway stations : _____

tracks: _____

freight: _____

dry goods: _____

hardware: _____

Language Activities:

1. **a)** What did Julilly mean when she thought about how "the white folks who'd helped them along the way were good and kind, but it wasn't the same."

   _____

   _____

   b) Why was there a difference for Julilly between good "white folks" and "colored folks"?

   _____

2. Julilly, Liza, Mammy Sally, Lester, and Adam are fictitious characters. They have been made up by the author. Do some research and write a paragraph to tell the story of a real slave who escaped into Canada. When you make a good copy on a clean sheet of paper, your teacher can put your class's biographies all together to make a special book about the true stories of real slaves who showed great courage.

 # Underground to Canada

By Barbara Smucker

Chapter 15

Before you read:

In this chapter, Julilly and Liza face fear again. Think of a time when you were afraid. What changes in your body did the fear cause?

_____

_____

_____

_____

Vocabulary:

Underground to Canada
By Barbara Smucker

Down

2. the code word for 'girl slaves'
4. the city in Ohio where Levi Coffin lives
5. a long, shallow container for animals to eat and drink from
7. someone who is against slavery
8. a star that led slaves north to Canada
9. a religion founded in Germany
14. what Mr. Ross pretends he's in the deep South hunting for
16. a person who is kept against their will and forced to do work

Across

1. the country north of the United States
3. the main character
6. a large crop farm
10. the people who assist runaway slaves to get into Canada
11. a bird with a distinct song
12. dogs used to track runaway people
13. a friend who helps Liza and Julilly
15. the state in which the Riley plantation is found
17. a religion that does not believe in slavery
18. an instrument that shows direction

Questions:

1. Where did Liza and Julilly hide?

_____

_____

2. Why did the sheriff want to search Jeb Brown's house?

_____

_____

3. List the steps in Julilly and Liza's journey after they leave Jeb Brown's house.

_____

_____

_____

4. How did Pal help the runaway slaves on the Underground Railway?

_____

_____

Underground to Canada

By Barbara Smucker

Language Activities:

1. Julilly states that "Ella and Jeb Brown are my friends forever", even though she has just met them and may never see them again.

   a) What do you think Julilly means by the word friend?

   _____

   _____

   b) What does the word friend mean to you?

   _____

   _____

2. Julilly repeatedly sings a song throughout the book:

   > When Israel was in Egypt's land
   > Let my people go
   > Oppressed so hard, they could not stand
   > Let my people go

   Do some research to find out what the reference to "Israel in Egypt's land" means.
   Hint: It is part of Hebrew history.

   _____

   _____

   _____

3. On a separate sheet, create a cover for the book Underground to Canada. Don't forget to add the title and the author.

Underground to Canada
By Barbara Smucker

Chapter 16

Before you read:

Julilly and Liza need to be hidden in the houses of the Underground Railroad when the slave hunters come searching for them. How would you hide two runaway slaves in your home?

_____

_____

_____

Vocabulary:

Draw each of these vocabulary words to show its meaning.

carriage

shawl

warrant

sheriff

locomotive

Quaker hat

Underground to Canada

By Barbara Smucker

Questions:

1. Name three physical features of Mr. Levi Coffin.

   _____

   _____

   _____

2. How did Catherine Levi hide Julilly and Liza when the slave catcher came to look for them?

   _____

   _____

   _____

3. What explanation did Levi Coffin give the slave catcher for his involvement in assisting slaves?

   _____

   _____

   _____

4. **a)** What did Catherine Levi give the girls when they left?

   _____

   b) Where did these gifts come from?

   _____

Underground to Canada
By Barbara Smucker

Language Activities:

1. Mr. Coffin follows his beliefs rather than the law.

   a) Can you think of an example in modern times when this might be a good thing to do?

   _____

   _____

   _____

   b) Can you think of an example when this might not be a good thing to do?

   _____

   _____

   _____

2. Why is there no slavery in Canada at the time of the novel?

   _____

   _____

Underground to Canada
By Barbara Smucker

Chapter 17

Before you read:

Julilly and Liza feel very special in their new sweaters; they've never had new clothes before. What clothes make you feel special?

_____

_____

_____

Vocabulary:

There are many words in this chapter that describe the sounds Julilly and Liza hear while in hiding. Some are adjectives, some are verbs, some are nouns. How many can you find? Try to find at least nine.

_____   _____   _____

_____   _____   _____

_____   _____   _____

Questions:

1. What were Levi Coffin's departing words to the children?

_____

2. How did Mr. Ross get out of prison?

_____

_____

3. What happened to Lester and Adam?

_____

_____

4. Why didn't Julilly ask about Mammy Sally?

_____

5. What does Julilly do in this chapter to show her unselfishness?

_____

6. Where is the *Mayflower* taking the girls?

_____

7. What is Mr. Ross going to do next?

_____

Language Activities:

1. What does Mr. Ross mean when he says, "injustice is the weapon of evil men".

_____

_____

_____

2. Write the plurals for the following nouns found in this chapter:

a) schooner _____   **b)** package   _____

c) person   _____   **d)** child   _____

e) sleeve   _____   **f)** moustache   _____

g) friend   _____   **h)** woman   _____

i) carriage   _____   **j)** tear   _____

Underground to Canada

By Barbara Smucker

Chapter 18

Before you read:

Julilly and Liza are very close to freedom. Can you think of a time when you expected something good to happen? Describe it, and how you felt.

_____

_____

_____

Vocabulary:

Choose the correct word to use in each of the following sentences.

trials	canvas	bobbed	lapping
refreshed	conductor	limp	dazzled

1. The _____ checked our tickets on the train.

2. After a good long sleep, we were _____ and ready to climb the mountain.

3. The sails were made with thick, heavy _____.

4. The light _____ as it hit the water, and I was glad I had sunglasses to wear.

5. Do you see how the waves are _____ against the shore?

6. The lettuce leaves were _____ and soft so the chef did not put them in the salad.

7. The champion swimmer's head _____ up and down as she made her way across the pool.

8. After so many _____, this small hardship seemed easy to overcome.

Underground to Canada

By Barbara Smucker

Questions:

Answer **True** or **False** for the following statements.

1. The Captain of the *Mayflower* risked his job to help slaves get to Canada. **T** or **F**

2. Julilly and Liza are going to Fort Malden where Lester lives. **T** or **F**

3. Julilly and Liza hid in a lifeboat. **T** or **F**

4. Slave hunters could take slaves back to their owners, no matter where in the United States they found them. **T** or **F**

5. A slave hunter received a reward for catching a runaway slave. **T** or **F**

6. Lake Erie is still on the border between United States and Canada. **T** or **F**

7. Julilly and Liza would rather drown in Lake Erie than be slaves again. **T** or **F**

Underground to Canada

By Barbara Smucker

Language Activities:

On the map of the United States and Canada, draw and label the following:

a) Vicksburg, Mississippi; Mississippi River; Appalachian Mountains; Covington, Kentucky; Cincinnati, Ohio; Lake Erie; Fort Malden, Upper Canada (now near Amherstburg); St. Catherine's, Upper Canada

b) Draw a line to trace the journey that Julilly and Liza have made from Mississippi.

c) Using the scale on the map, calculate the distance they have traveled to Canada.

_____

Upper Canada
(Now Ontario)

Ohio

West Virginia

Virginia

Kentucky

Tennessee

Mississippi

0	400 km
0	300 Miles

Underground to Canada
By Barbara Smucker

Chapter 19

Before you read:

Imagine you are Julilly or Liza. You have just arrived in Canada, and are no longer a slave, but free. What would you do?

_____

_____

_____

Vocabulary:

Draw a straight line to match the word to its definition. Remember to use a straight edge, such as a ruler.

a) cluster	historical name for Ontario
b) burnished	fear
c) Upper Canada	person who carries luggage at a hotel
d) apprehension	a group of trees
e) shrub	a gathering
f) suspense	polished and shiny
g) porter	small, woody plant
h) grove	uncertainty

Underground to Canada

By Barbara Smucker

Questions:

1. What does Liza do when she arrives on the Canadian shores of Lake Erie?

   _____

2. Even though they are free, Liza still wants to hide in the bushes. Why?

   _____

   _____

3. Ezra Wilson tells them many things about Canada, and its hardships. List them.

   _____

   _____

   _____

   _____

   _____

   _____

   _____

4. What are Mammy Sally's plans for the future?

   _____

   _____

Underground to Canada

By Barbara Smucker

Language Activities:

1. In this chapter, and throughout the novel, the author uses many **similes** – a comparison using **like** or **as** – to make her descriptions interesting. Find six similies from this chapter.

   _____

   _____

   _____

   _____

   _____

   _____

2 a) Both Mammy Sally and Lester stand tall, and keep their heads held high. What does this tell you about them?

   _____

   _____

   b) If a person keeps their head down, or walks hunched over, what might this tell you about them?

   _____

   _____

3. With a classmate, discuss how the history of slavery has affected people of African descent living in North America today. Try to think of at least two things.

   _____

   _____

   _____

   _____

   _____

Answer Key

Chapter 1: *(page 9)*

Vocabulary: plan/ta/tion, o/ver/se/er, Vir/gin/ia, mel/o/dy, quar/ters, tra/der, Mas/sa, chirp/ing

Questions:

1. Master
2. Answers may vary (e.g., the song spoke of freedom and might encourage slaves to run away).
3. The Hensens were selling their plantation and moving North. Mr. Hensen was old and sick and had to go to the hospital in Richmond.
4. about being sold, separated, and sent to the 'deep South'
5. June Lilly

Language Activities:

1. United States, specifically on a slave plantation in West Virginia, during the second half of the 19th century.
2. Answers may vary.

Chapter 2: *(page 11)*

Vocabulary: calloused-roughened skin; hobble-to limp along; mulatto-a person who has one black parent and one white parent; buttermilk-liquid left after milk has been made into butter; hoecake-a small cake made from corn

Questions:

1. wakes up the slaves
2. sowbelly (bacon), hoecakes, and buttermilk
3. buying slaves
4. a) he pulled back her lips and looked at her teeth
   b) like an animal (horse)
5. Willie, Julilly, Ben, Adam, Lester, and some other children
6. Answers may vary (e.g., to stop them from running away or causing trouble).

Language Activities:

1. Answers may vary.
2. The word is used by the fat man to describe the baby boy he buys. (This is opportunity to discuss word usage; words when used in a negative way over time will become negative. It is the way it is used, not necessarily the origin of the word, that is so negative.)
3. Answers may vary.

Chapter 3: *(page 14)*

Vocabulary: Answers may vary.

Questions:

1. waterfall
2. the chains rubbed and cut the skin
3. He was not a slave but a free person. He was paid for his work.
4. a gourd full of water
5. Answers may vary (e.g., he did not want them to encourage his slaves to run away; he did not like to be forced to think about the wrong he was doing to these people).

Language Activities:

1. Answers may vary.
2. a) Answers may vary (e.g., wide brimmed hats, bonnets, aprons, simple clothes).
   b) Answers may vary (e.g., simplicity, faith, peace, equality, education).

Chapter 4: *(page 17)*

Vocabulary: 1. racket 2. wanted 3. unbearable 4. ringing 5. puffy

Questions:

1. She sang to them.
2. Answers may vary (e.g., it was harder because the men could not lift their chains through the mud and the children were wet and uncomfortable).
3. She jumped off the wagon and helped the men walk.
4. a) Answers may vary (e.g., he was proud of her).
   b) Answers may vary (e.g., this made Julilly feel proud of herself).

Language Activities:

1. Answers may vary (e.g., thin, strong, high-held, spreading, bruised, muddy, wet, warm, good, firm).
2. Answers may vary.

Extension:

Answers may vary, however it is generally agreed to originate within American slave culture.

Chapter 5: *(page 20)*

Vocabulary:

1. drawled 2. billows 3. fragrance 4. plume 5. sprouted 6. sullen 7. parading 8. sagged 9. appraised 10. pillars

Questions:

1. Mississippi
2. Mr. Sims. He is the overseer (boss of the slaves).
3. Answers may vary (e.g., they are unhappy and do not like newcomers; new slaves do not make their lives easier; they have been mistreated so much that they have lost the ability to be kind to others; they are afraid).

Language Activities:

1. Answers may vary.

Chapter 6: *(page 22)*

Vocabulary: 1. frail 2. gaiety 3. relaxed 4. blunt 5. glistening

Questions:

1. kind, sad, beaten and crippled
2. She was beaten by Sims when she tried to runaway.
3. children being fed from a trough like animals
4. Breakfast: corn cake and water; Lunch: one corn cake, one strip of bacon

Language Activities:

1. that a person's worth is about what is on the inside, not the color of their skin
2. Answers may vary.

Chapter 7: (page 25)

Vocabulary:

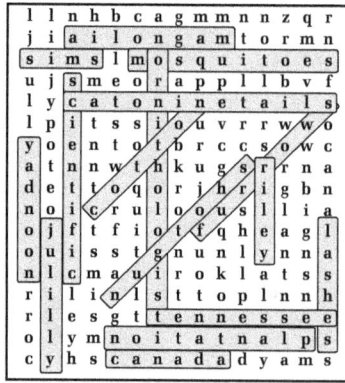

Questions:

1. 100 pounds
2. they were whipped
3. folks in Canada would skin a black man, and eat black children; that it is so cold that people should not live there; no crops can grow except black-eyed peas
4. studying birds
5. Answers may vary (e.g., she was fascinated by his appearance; he was from Canada; she had a feeling something good was going to happen).

Language Activities:

1. Answers may vary (e.g., zoologist, entomologist, radiologist, cardiologist, biologist, technologist, hydrologist).
2. Answers may vary. (This is an opportunity to discuss how we can all sometimes discriminate for reasons that are superficial; this can assist people to identify what aspects of themselves lead to discriminatory thoughts, and thus prevent them. Not trusting people who are simply different is natural, but usually unfounded. People sometimes learn prejudice from their parents; people sometimes are prejudice because of their own insecurities – putting others down makes them feel better about themselves.)
3. Answers may vary.

Chapter 8: (page 28)

Vocabulary:

a) awakened   b) a small, sudden flash of light   c) moving swiftly and lightly   d) shine irregularly   e) not enough   f) neat and tidy
g) particular way of speaking   h) skinny   i) jerk   j) rough sounding

Questions:

1. cotton
2. Answers may vary (e.g., they sensed something unusual was going to happen; it was a change in routine and they were fearful of anything new).
3. The North Star was in the direction of Canada, where black people were free.
4. She go where she pleased; get paid for her work; not get whipped.
5. run away to Canada

Language Activities:

1. Answers may vary (e.g., *Verbs:* picking, weighing, flicker, trudged, swung; *Adverbs:* more, too, far, mighty, barely; *Adjectives:* big, shade, cold, black, sparse; *Nouns:* kettle, smile, hand, daddy, sky)

Chapter 9: (page 30)

Vocabulary: a) disturbance   b) scavenge   c) promise   d) serious   e) pulled tight   f) make free   g) intelligence

Questions:

1. Answers may vary.
2. She was shocked.
3. a) She pretended Liza was too weak to hold it and lifted it up for her.
   b) So the others would not look at them and notice Liza behaving strangely.
4. They were to meet Lester who would take them to a meeting in the woods.
5. He shook their hands warmly.

Language Activities:

1. a) On Sundays, Julilly and Liza washed their clothes at the Riley plantation.   b) When Bessie fell asleep, the girls met Lester in the woods.
   c) Will the girls meet Mr. Ross to talk about Canada?
2. Answers may vary (e.g., this implies that the slaves are objects, not people; it is a good, noble, and brave thing that Mr. Ross is doing by acting opposite to this idea).

Chapter 10: (page 33)

Vocabulary: 1. knapsack   2. grumble   3. astonished   4. meager   5. midday   6. jovial   7. lank   8. serene

Questions:

1. firefly: "flickering turned to hot, bright sparks"; grasshoppers: "eyes bulged"; cicadas: "cackled, and cackled, and CACKLED"
2. She was afraid it would stop them from leaving on Saturday night because they wouldn't be able to see the North Star in the sky.
3. to make it harder for the bloodhounds to trace their scent
4. two dollar bills, a knife, cold meat, bread; Julilly and Liza also received a shirt and pair of pants
5. Answers may vary (e.g., no they didn't sleep well because they were nervous and they could hear bloodhounds after them).

Language Activities:

1. Answers may vary (e.g., she walked with Liza even though she slowed them down; she rested when Liza needed to even though it would slow them down; she didn't wake Liza to keep watch with her).
2. a) hoecakes, winter shoes, drinking gourd   b) Answers may vary.
3. Answers may vary.

Chapter 11: (page 36)

Before you read:

1. a) 1850   b) People who assisted runaway slaves would be fined and imprisoned, no matter where in the United States they were.

Vocabulary: **a)** quiver   **b)** jog   **c)** plod   **d)** clop   **e)** croak   **f)** lap   **g)** lapse   **h)** scuffle

Questions:
1. They will see a sign.
2. He was a kind slaveowner.
3. friends with a friend
4. They could go to jail and be fined $1000
5. He had been caught for helping slaves and put in prison.
6. He met them on the road, hid them in a wagon covered in hay, and told them he was bringing them to an old farmhouse where there was food for them.

Language Activities:
1. Answers may vary (e.g., minute, excuse, record).
2. Answers may vary.

Chapter 12: *(page 39)*
Vocabulary:
a) dark suffix – ness   **b)** cross suffix – ly   **c)** tangle prefix – un   **d)** thought suffix – ful   **e)** nerve suffix – ous
f) abolition suffix – ist, s   **g)** free suffix – dom   **h)** lap suffix – ng

Questions:
1. a compass, some food, and instructions on where to go next
2. east
3. venison, bread, cheese
4. Lester and Adam went across the river to find food. The bloodhounds chased their scent, they were caught and put back in chains.

Language Activities: Answers may vary.

Chapter 13: *(page 41)*
Before you read: east
Vocabulary: craggy, crippled, despair, fragrance, ragged, scant, shallow, stern, sweet
Questions:
1. 3,8,5,1,4,2,6,7
2. rows of neat, small cabins; boxed in gardens; bright flowers; women in long skirts with their hair in buns; children playing

Language Activities:
1. Answers may vary.
2. **a)** Answers may vary (e.g., threatening and don't want them near them; helpful and kind).
   b) Answers may vary (e.g., they are afraid; have strong beliefs or faith).
3. Answers may vary.

Chapter 14: *(page 44)*
Vocabulary: **a)** giggled   **b)** weak   **c)** fancy   **d)** sluggish   **e)** modern   **f)** silly
Questions:
1. They dug a place under a rock, and hid behind tree limbs.
2. He too was a slave, and gave them his only food for the day.
3. Walk north until they hear the Ohio River, and then go to the house on the river bank with one candle lit in the window.
4. Answers may vary (e.g., it was their only chance).
5. **a)** A system of people that assist slaves get to Canada where they can be free.
   b) railway stations – homes where slaves are hidden
   tracks – the roads followed to get to Canada
   freight – runaway slaves
   dry goods – women runaway slaves
   hardware – men runaway slaves

Language Activities:
1. **a)** Answers may vary (e.g., She felt more comfortable and at home with them; they understood her better).
   b) Answers may vary (e.g., She could trust the black people more not to hurt her).
2. Answers may vary.

Chapter 15: *(page 47)*
Vocabulary:

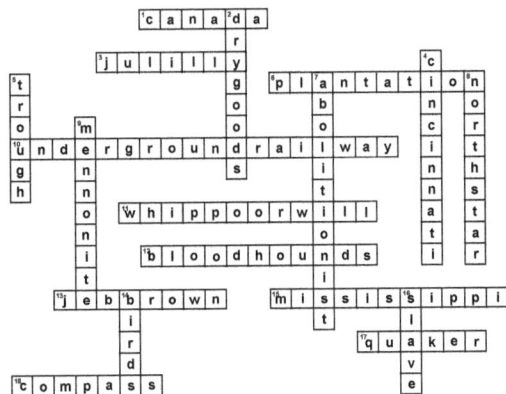

Questions:
1. on the roof
2. He knew Jeb Brown helped slaves, so the slaves he was looking for could be there.
3. followed Ella to the river; Jeb rowed them across in a rowboat; another man led them to a cart; they were put in a large cart and were on their way to Cincinnati
4. He barked when people were coming to warn them.

Language Activities:

1. **a)** Answers may vary (e.g., someone who helps you when you are in trouble; someone you feel comfortable with).
   b) Answers may vary.
2. Answers may vary (e.g., the Israelites were kept as slaves by the Egyptian people for around 400 years; Moses led them out of Egypt into Israel).

Chapter 16: *(page 50)*
Questions:
1. Answers may vary (e.g., gaunt, blue eyes, tall).
2. She put them between the bedding, then put a smooth cover on top, so you could not see them.
3. Levi Coffin said that he believed in the Bible and its command to feed and clothe the poor and hungry; and that the Bible did not distinguish on the grounds of skin color.
4. **a)** new clothes and a new sweater each, made with bright blue wool   **b)** the sewing circle of the Quaker meeting
Language Activities:
1. **a)** Answers may vary (e.g., when the law results in people being hurt or treated unfairly, for example the Taliban laws in Afghanistan that say that girls can't go to school).
   b) Answers may vary (e.g., when laws are in place to protect people (most laws today are like this)).
2. Canada is ruled by Queen Victoria, who does not believe in slavery.

Chapter 17: *(page 53)*
Vocabulary:
1. Answers may vary (e.g., pattered, hissing, screech, creaked, clanged, clicking, humming, rattled, banged, muffled, ring, husky, trilled).
Questions:
1. "God bless you both."
2. The slave who he was charged with helping returned and walked into the courtroom.
3. They escaped to Canada. Lester had a job; Adam died from blood poisoning.
4. She was afraid the news was bad, and didn't want to hear it.
5. She gave Liza water to drink first, even though she was very thirsty herself.
6. Across Lake Erie to Fort Malden, Canada.
7. Go back South to free more slaves.
Language Activities:
1. Answers may vary (e.g., injustice helps those that do wrong).
2. **a)** schooners   **b)** packages   **c)** people   **d)** children   **e)** sleeves   **f)** moustaches   **g)** friends
   h) women   **i)** carriages   **j)** tears

Chapter 18: *(page 55)*
Vocabulary: 1. conductor   2. refreshed   3. canvas   4. dazzled   5. lapping   6. limp   7. bobbed   8. trials
Questions: 1. T   2. F   3. T   4. T   5. T   6. T   7. T
Language Activities:
1. Approximate distance traveled: 1530 miles (2450 km).

Chapter 19: *(page 58)*

Vocabulary:
1. **a)** a gathering   **b)** polished and shiny   **c)** historical name for Ontario   **d)** fear   **e)** small, woody plant
   f) uncertainty   **g)** person who carries luggage at a hotel   **h)** a group of trees
Questions:
1. kneels down and prays
2. Answers may vary (e.g., she is used to hiding and it hasn't sunk in yet that she doesn't need to be afraid).
3. colored folks work very hard, have food to eat but not very good food, and warm dry place to live, no one can read, white folks don't want colored folks in same school, white school has more books, paper, more desks, better building
4. To buy a house and live with Julilly and Liza.
Language Activities:
1. Answers may vary (e.g., "idea struck her like a bolt of lightning", "his hair bushed out from his head like a grey and black speckled frame":, "there was a burnished glow about it [the sun], like the ripened skin of a red apple", "it's [Canada] like heaven here", "the beatings and chains hadn't crushed him down like a snake", "being with Mammy Sally again was like shifting a hundred-pound sack of cotton from her back and just taking on a two-pound load").
2. **a)** Answers may vary (e.g., she is proud and confident in her value as a person).
   b) Answers may vary (e.g., he/she is not confident and does not feel good about themself).
3. Answers may vary (This question can lead to discussions about the impact of mistreatment on people's self-esteem; the questions of prejudice existing today and whether its roots can be traced to slavery or whether it is something that exists everywhere where there are people living together who are different; whether inequality can set up economic situations where the rich get richer and the poor get poorer; and what influence heritage has on people in general – pride, sense of belonging, community, trust, etc.).